A LITTLE TOUCH OF CLOSE-UP MAGIC

By

Michael Little

Copyright©2016 Michael Little

For Intermediate & Advanced Magicians

Recommended books for beginners:

Royal Road to Card Magic by Frederick Braue and Jean Hugard

The New Modern Coin Magic by J.B. BoBo

(For beginners: Please read first the bonus section of basic card sleights in the back of booklet.)

Special Thanks

I would like to give thanks to most of my magic friends, who have given me great feedback and encouragement throughout the years.

Chip Romero

Jason Crain

Perry Vincent

Steve Daly

Don Hahn

Darin Martineau

Randall Ford Sager

Allan Ackerman

Contents

Introduction

What really inspired me to write this is to share and inspire others about how I overcame my obstacles. I was born with a mild cerebral palsy on my left hand. I remember as an amateur magician, I felt very discouraged after learning certain sleights that required the use of my left hand. However, after learning about Rene Lavand's techniques and his successful career, I gained confidence to continue as a close-up magician. Throughout the years, I've been learning new methods for an effects that I liked. That's why I've always liked to be challenged, in order to become a better close-up magician. The effects in this booklet have been worked hard for many years, for which I'm very pleased. I hope you enjoy them. Thanks!

Michael Little

Glass with a Twist of Coin (coin through glass routine)

Effect: A coin penetrates through the bottom of a long narrowed drinking glass. As a surprise ending, the coin magically grows into a jumbo coin while it slides out of the glass.

The coin-through-glass routine has many variations, such as loading an extra coin on the ledge of the open glass with a card case covering it, using a gimmick card case, or simply throwing the same coin into the open glass.

Secret/Setup

Place a dab of magician's wax on center of the card case with the playing cards insert inside. Close the flap. Be sure not to use too much magician's wax, because you don't want to draw too much attention to the dab. A long, narrowed drinking glass (with its diameter smaller than the width of the card case) is recommended, since it will eliminate the idea that you secretly tossed the coin into the glass. Two half dollars and one jumbo half dollar are used: One half dollar is finger palmed in the right hand while the other is inside of your outer right jacket pocket along with the jumbo half dollar.

Method

To Start:

Option 1: You can preset the routine by simply sticking one of the half dollars onto the magician's wax from the center of the card case (be careful not to press the coin too hard on the wax). Just be sure that this side faces down on the table so you don't expose it to the spectators.

Option 2: Finger palm the half dollar with the right hand while showing both sides of the playing card case (with playing cards inside). Rotate the card case with your right index finger so that it ends wax-side up **(See Figure #1)**. This is placed squarely (and secretly) onto the coin from your finger palm position. Then, rotate the card case again and place it on aside of the table.

Step 1: Arch your left hand over the rim, so you can grip and lift both of the card case and glass from the table. Be sure to face slightly to the right, so the spectators don't see the hidden half dollar from inside of the glass. Reach into your right pocket, take out the other half dollar, and hold it between your right second finger and thumb. Show and tap the half dollar on the bottom of the glass two times. After the second count, execute a one handed coin sleeve into your right jacket sleeve before you hit the bottom glass with your right palm (Dr. E. M. Roberts Sleeve Method, from J.B. Bobo's New Modern Coin Magic, pg. 107). The motion is similar to snapping your fingers, while shooting the half dollar right into your right jacket sleeve. At the same time, when you tap the bottom of glass with your right open palm, the inertia should allow the hidden half dollar that is stuck onto the card case (with magician's wax) to drop into the glass. This will create the illusion that a coin has penetrated through the glass. Keep the half dollar laying on the inside of the glass as you turn, and place it on the table with its rim to the right.

Step 2: Drop your right hand down to allow the half dollar drop onto your right fingers from the inside of your right jacket sleeve. Use the same hand to pick up the card case along with hidden half dollar, and place both into your right jacket pocket. Then, steal the jumbo half dollar and grip it in a curl position before you take your right hand out of the pocket. To do this, grip the jumbo half dollar on its edge in a vertical position with your right third finger and open palm **(See Figure #2)**. This allows you to separate your fingers, so you can have access to grip the rim of the glass **(See Figure #3)**.

Note: I recommend having the glass near at the edge of the table close to you, so there is a short

distance between the glass and your right pocket after you take your right hand (concealing the jumbo coin) out of the pocket. There should be no hesitation while you pick up the glass with the right hand. Be careful of the angles, since this type of regular coin to jumbo coin inflation illusion has to be executed in a timely manner.

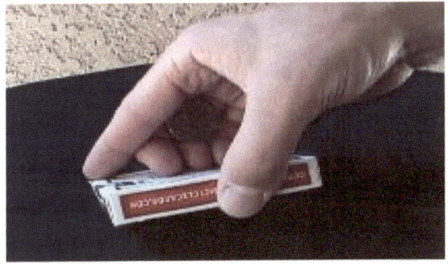

Figure #1

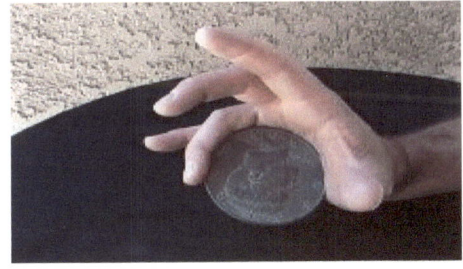

Figure # 2

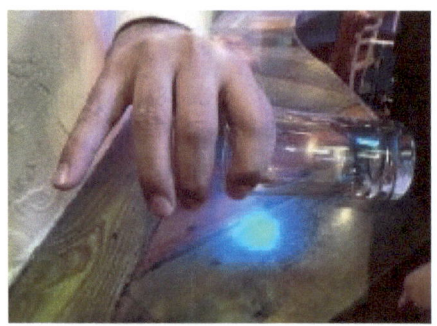

Figure #3

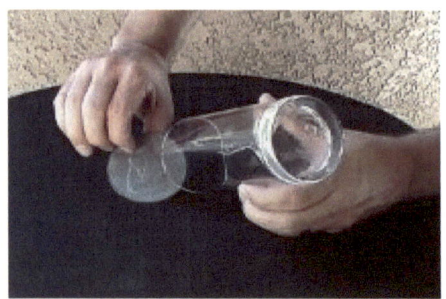

Figure #4

Step 3: Tilt the glass slightly, allowing the half dollar to slide down and into finger palm as soon as it falls out. Simultaneously, loosen the grip with your right third finger, allowing the jumbo half dollar to fall onto the table **(See Figure #4)**.

Step 4: Immediately, lay the card case aside, and grab the rim of glass with your left hand. Finally, tap the jumbo half dollar on the glass with the right hand while concealing the regular half dollar size.

The Metamorphic Dollar

A visual one handed transformation from a dollar coin to a bill.

Secret/Setup

Fold a dollar bill into eighths and back clip between the first two fingers. Rest the dollar coin onto the

first and second two fingers to cover the edge of the dollar bill **(See Figure #5 & # 6).**

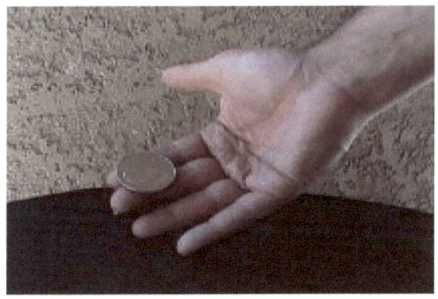

Figure #5

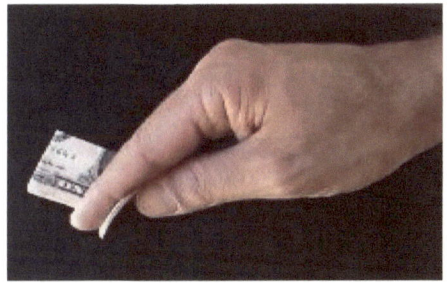

Figure # 6 (Be sure to hold the dollar coin with the right thumb as you move it)

Note: Be sure to perform with your left side shoulder facing the audience.

Method

You could start off with the dollar bill in a finger palm position as you hold the dollar coin with the left hand. As you turn with the side of your left shoulder toward the spectators, transfer the dollar bill to a back finger clip from the side of your leg before placing the dollar coin onto the left fingers. This should be done smoothly.

Step 1: While you slightly wave your open right hand up and down with your right thumb pressing against the dollar coin **(Same as Figure # 6)**, reveal the dollar bill by gripping it between with your right thumb and first finger as you classic palm the dollar coin with its second, third, and fourth fingers, which are used to press it against the palm. It's important to slightly tilt its wrist to the right, so you don't expose the dollar coin from the palm of your right hand after the transformation **(See Figure # 7)**.

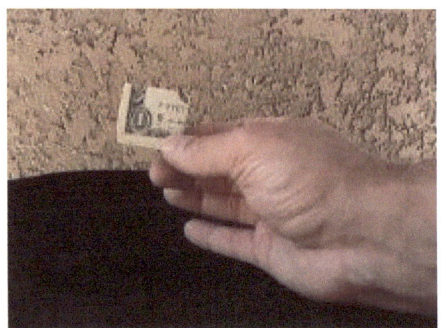

Figure # 7 (from audience's view)

Step 2: As soon as the dollar bill is revealed, reach over with your left hand to unfold the bill. When the bill is unfolded halfway, secretly release the dollar coin from classic palm and hide it behind the bill **(See Figure # 8).** When you turn your right hand around to show the other side of bill, slide the dollar coin inward toward the palm with your fingers (almost off the bill). **(See Figure # 9).**

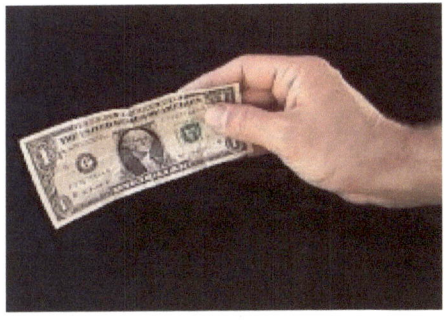

Figure # 8

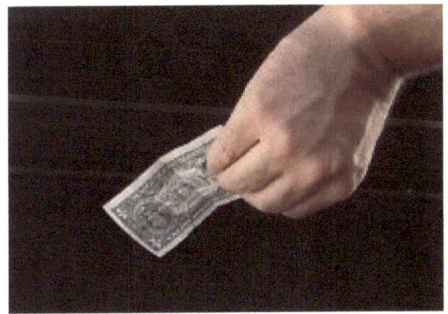

Figure # 9

Note: This should be done quickly and smoothly, in order to create a nice visual change.

The Marked Card (color changing deck routine)

Effect: A color changing deck routine where a card is chosen from a red backed deck and replaced. The magician holds the deck up high with the faces toward the spectators, and attempts to find the selection without looking at the faces. After the magician successfully finds the selected card and out jogging it, he explains that selection is the only marked card from the rest of the pack. He turns over and shows that the red back of the selected card now has its selection name written across with a black permanent marker. Finally, the rest of the deck is turned over to show that the backs of all the other cards have changed to blue.

There are several variations of the color changing deck routine. This routine is an adaptation of the "And the spectator blew" from *Card Magic* by John Northern Hillard's published in 1945. It's an effect where not only the selected card magically turns face down, but it also changed to a blue backed. The rest of the deck also changed to blue.

Secret/Setup

Use a blue-backed deck and three red backed cards: one indifferent card and the other two duplicate cards. On the back of one of the duplicate cards, the name of that same card is written across with a black permanent marker. For example, two duplicate cards of the ace of hearts will be used. With a black permanent marker, write the "ace of hearts" on one of the red backed ace of hearts.

Note: Be sure to discard the duplicate blue backed cards from the blue- backed deck: ace of hearts and whatever indifferent card you choose.

From the top of the deck down, place the regular ace of hearts with the red- backed indifferent card second from the top. The ace of hearts is the first top card. Insert the other red backed ace of hearts with its name written across its back face down into the deck about a quarter from the top. There's no need to worry about exposing its back during the beginning of the routine, since you will do a Hindu Shuffle Force while dealing off chunks of cards one at a time. Place the deck into a red backed card case.

Method

Step 1: Take the "red-backed" deck out of the card case. Spread the cards between the hands to show its faces, but be careful not to show the duplicate cards (two ace of hearts, especially the preset card near top of the deck). Proceed by squaring the deck face up and perform a Hindu Shuffle by showing the top red-backed card ace of hearts continuously (Hindu Color Change). While you are doing this, simply show the red-backed a couple of times during the shuffle, rather than overstating the idea that you have a red-backed deck. When you have approximately twelve cards remaining in the right hand, place those face up cards squared on the table. Then, place the face up pile, held in the left hand, on top of the tabled face up pile.

Step 2: Repeat the Hindu Shuffle. This time, ask the spectator to stop you, while you do the Hindu Shuffle to force the top regular ace of hearts (Hindu Shuffle Force). After the spectator stops you, turn your right hand and use your thumb to deal off the face down ace of hearts onto the table. Then, place the squared face up pile (the same pile you dealt the ace of hearts from) aside, and place the face up pile from the left hand on top of the tabled face up pile. You are doing this because you are not showing the color of the backs yet. Show the back of the selected card (ace of hearts) and place it face up on the bottom of deck. It's important to take your time when showing the back of the ace of hearts, since you want the spectators to remember that there was nothing written on it at the end of the routine.

Step 3: Do a Double Undercut by transferring the ace of hearts to the top of the deck **(See Figure # 10, 11, & 12 for sequence of transferring the ace of hearts from bottom to top of deck).** Arch your left hand over the face up deck while keeping a flesh thumb break between the ace of hearts and the second bottom card.

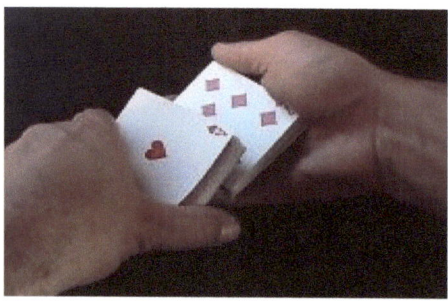

.

Figure #10 (split the deck while holding a flesh thumb break above the ace of hearts).

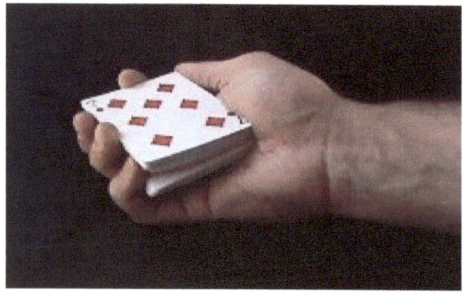

Figure # 11 (from a flesh thumb break to a little finger break under the ace of hearts, which is now the top card of the 7 of diamonds pile. Cut the deck back to the original order).

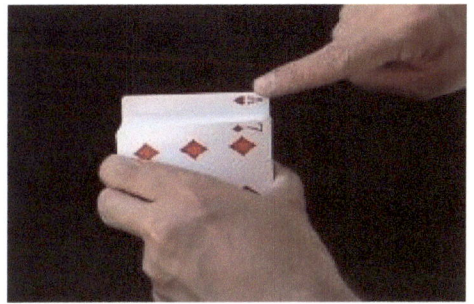

Figure # 12 (right index finger showing the ace of hearts is now top of the deck).

Step 4: Hold the deck at about chest level, with the faces toward the spectator. Explain that you will attempt to find the selected card without seeing the faces. Thumb spread the cards with your right thumb from the bottom to top of deck. As you do this, you can spot the written red- backed ace of hearts while looking directly at the spectator (An inspiration of one of Mike Roger's routine). Stop at that card and out-jogged it (stick out halfway from center of deck). Meanwhile, secretly transfer any blue-backed card from the center of the deck with its thumb to the top of the deck, in order to cover the top two red-backed cards **(See Figure # 13).** Without showing the rest of the blue-backed cards yet, strip the ace of hearts out of the spread and place it face up onto the table. Square and keep the deck face up.

Step 5: Explain that you were able to find the selection without seeing the faces because their card is marked. Turn the card over to show the name of the chosen card, which is now written on its back. Say, "It's the only marked card from the entire deck". Turn the rest of the deck to reveal that it is now a blue deck.

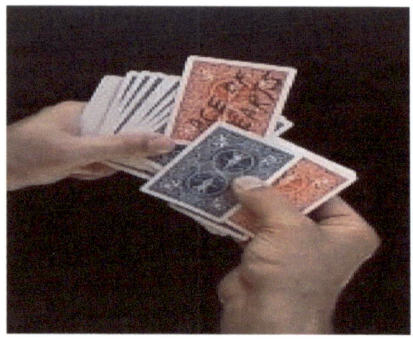

Figure # 13 (from performer's view, the faces are spread in front of audience).

A Gambler's Dream

 This routine is an inspiration from a card effect I witnessed from Alfonso, a great close–up magician from San Diego. Allan Ackerman once told me that he does the best bottom palm in the world. It's a quick visual effect where any named four of a kind (I chose the jacks) was taken out of the deck and they immediately changed into four aces, then back to the jacks between his hands, while the rest of the deck was placed on the table. The routine, I believe, is called Punch in, Punch out. Of course, the concept and handling of this routine is different than his, but I love the idea of performing a color change with more than one card, especially a five card poker hand in the hands(like a royal flush) while the rest of deck is placed onto the table.

Effect: Five indifferent cards turned to a straight flush of the same suit (spades), then to a royal flush between the hands.

Secret/Setup

Method: There's a fifteen card stack set up from the bottom of the deck: any indifferent four red number cards, ace of spades, rest for straight flush: two of spades, three of spades, four of spades, five of spades, rest for royal flush: ten of spades, jack of spades, queen of spades, king of spades, and two duplicate jokers. Make sure that both of the jokers are facing the same direction. **(See Figure # 14 for setup display).**

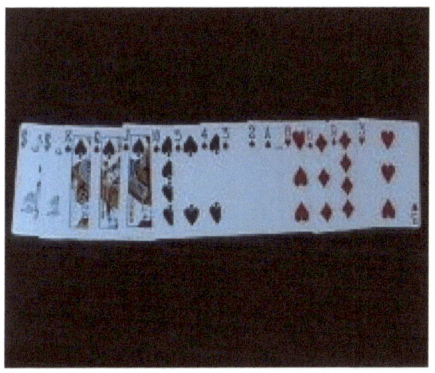

Figure # 14

Method

 Step 1: Hold the deck high and face up toward you, so the spectators don't see the stack. Thumb spread the cards, keeping a little finger break between the duplicate jokers. Re-squared the deck before lowering your hands. Hold the deck face up with the right hand in a gambler's dealing position while the break. Arch the left hand over the block and pick up the fourteen card stack with its thumb on the inner side and the first two fingers on the outer side of the stack.

Note: Be sure to tilt the back of your left hand toward the spectators, so they don't see the depth of the packet, which you are apparently showing as being only five cards.

Step 2: Now, you are going to do Edward Marlo's ATFUS (Anytime Face-Up Switch). To do this, hold the rest of the deck face up in a gambler's dealing position with the right hand. The second joker from the face of deck is shown to the spectators. With the left hand, obtain thumb break between the king of spades and the other joker from the bottom of the left-hand packet. Use your right thumb to peel off the first four indifferent red cards from the right side of the packet. Transfer them to underneath the bottom joker of the packet, but keep them slightly side jogged while keeping a flesh thumb break on the joker **(See Figure # 15)**.

Step 3: As you square the five cards from underneath the ace the spades, secretly drop all indifferent red cards, including the first joker onto the face of the deck. You will now end up having nine cards in the left-hand packet: ace (bottom of face packet), two of spades, three of spades, four of spades, five of spades, ten of spades, jack of spades, queen of spades, and the king of spades. Again, be careful not to show its depth of the left-hand packet.

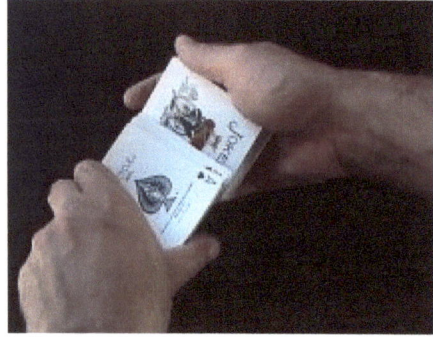

Figure # 15 (A view from above).

Note: Because you are using duplicate jokers, it will eliminate the idea that you've dropped the cards on the face of the deck, since a same joker from the bottom of the deck was apparently shown at all times.

Step 3: Place the deck face down on the table with the right hand while still holding the left-hand packet with the left hand. Now, you are going to reveal a straight flush with the same suit: ace, two, three, four, and five of spades. Hold the packet in a gambler's dealing position with the right hand. Thumb count the cards one by one to the left hand, but keep the block of five cards as one with the right hand (the five of spades with the rest of the remaining royal flush behind it). Four cards should be spread from the left hand, which will use them to screen the small packet held in your right hand. **(See Figure #16).**

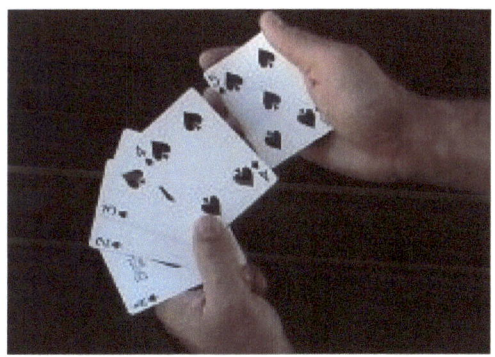

Figure #16

Note: Be careful not to tilt the right-hand packet sideways, so the spectators don't see the extra cards behind the five of spades. This should be done in a timely manner without any hesitation.

Step 5: Recount the cards back to the original order on top of the five of spades. After recounting the four of spades back on top of the five of spades, buckle under these two cards with your right little finger before you continue recounting the rest of the straight flush back onto the five of spades. Use the rest of the spread to screen the move **(See Figure # 17)**. Now, you will have a break between the packets of the straight flush (ace, two, three, four, and five of spades) and the remaining royal flush (ten, jack, queen, and king of spades).

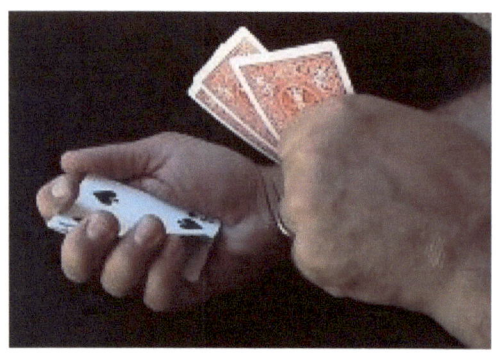

Figure # 17 (A view from behind the spread).

Step 6: With the left hand, arch over and Biddle Grip its squared packet of the straight flush. Transfer the block of the remaining royal flush over the ace of spades (with its block) with the right hand. Simultaneously, spread to the left with all right fingers from underneath, so the royal flush can be revealed in this order between your hands: Ace to King **(See Figure # 18).** Square the rest of the royal flush cards. Turn packet face down and drop it on top of the deck to finish.

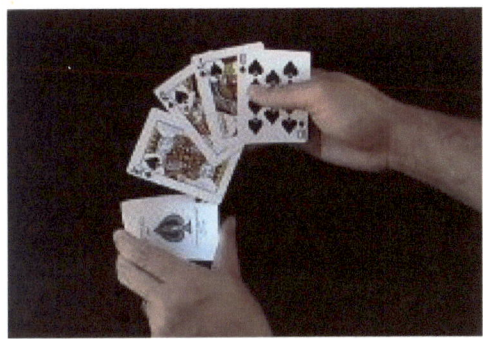

Figure #18

"King"aroos (an assembly routine)

Effect: An assembly routine, in which three kings vanish from three first dealt piles and join the leader king from the dealer's hand. Instantly, they magically jumped back to the piles.

This routine is an adaptation and inspiration of Allan Ackerman's Finally Unassembled from his book, *Las Vegas Kardma.*

Secret/Setup

From the top of the deck, set up the cards in this order: jack of spades, jack of diamonds. From the bottom of the deck, setup the kings in this order: king of hearts (fourth position from bottom), king of diamonds, king of clubs, and king of spades. Hold the deck face up with the left hand in a gambler's dealing position.

Method

Step 1: Spread the bottom six cards and catch a left finger break under the sixth card while re-squaring the cards. Turn the rest of the deck face down with the right hand while gripping the block of six cards with the left hand arched over it, so the face up block of four kings and two indifferent cards(underneath the kings) are now on top of the deck with the left finger break under it. Then, you will do a Multiple Turnover. Spread the first three kings to show all four of them without reversing the count. Re-square them and turn over the entire block of six cards face down on top of the deck **(See Figure # 19 & 20)**. Deal the four cards face down on the table from left to right, with the fourth card toward you like you are dealing a poker hand: a T formation **(See Figure # 21)**. The king of hearts is on your right and the king of diamonds is toward you, which will be known as a leader card.

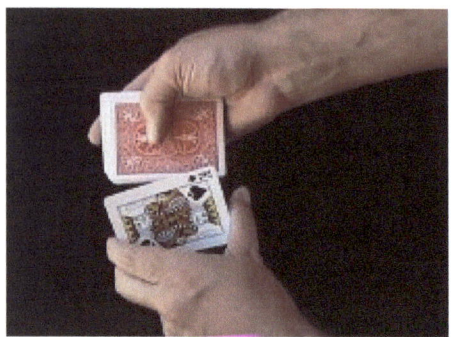

Figure # 19 (as you rotate the deck face down)

19

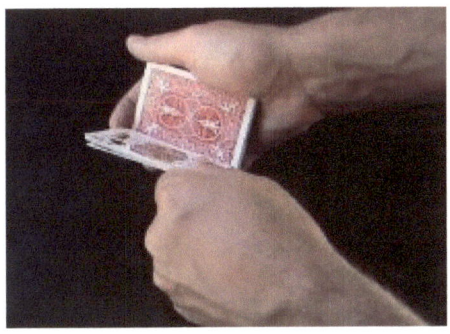

Figure # 20

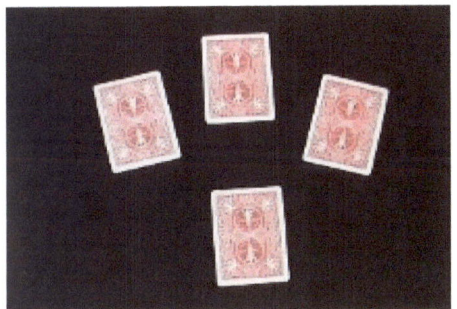

Figure # 21

Step 2: Count the top three cards from top of the deck to the left hand one at a time. When you reverse count back to the original order onto the top of the deck, add an additional card, but keep a little finger break under the packet of four cards. With the left hand arch over, pick up the packet of four cards squared, and place it on top of the leader card (king of diamonds).

For the card on the right of the T formation, spread the top three cards and transfer to the left hand from the top of deck. Then, reverse count the cards back on top of the deck one at a time, but keep a little finger break under the first dealt card. Pick up three cards above the break with the left hand and place them squared on top of the right card of the T formation (king of hearts). You are not adding or displacing a card. You are only using three cards to add onto the right card.

For the middle card of the T formation (apparently a king), spread the top three cards and transfer to the left hand. Reverse count the cards on top of the deck one at a time, but keep a little finger break above the first dealt card right before you continue counting the last two cards. Use the left hand to arch over the packet of two cards above the break. Place them squared on top of the middle card, apparently placing three cards.

Repeat the previous method you did for the middle card for the left card of the T formation.

At this point, you have apparently placed three indifferent cards on top of the leader, middle, and left king of the T formation one at a time. The right king card is the only one that has three indifferent cards.

Step 3: Now, you explain that you will attempt to make the three kings disappear and join with the leader king, which is the card nearest to you. Pick up the left packet of the T formation and perform an Elmsley Count, counting three cards as four. You are counting back the first card along with the third as you clear off the second card. To the spectators, it appears that you have counted the first king to the top of the packet. Turn over the top card of the packet to show that you disappeared the first king. Then, turn over and spread the rest of cards. Lay these three face down cards on the table to the left, in the same positon of the T formation.

Repeat the same method for the middle packet.

For the right packet, do an actual four card Elmsley Count to transfer the king of hearts to the second position from top of the packet, so you can show an indifferent top face card, in order to show that the third king has vanished from the packet. Turn the rest of cards face up with the right hand and spread count the cards. Hold the bottom two cards as a double, in order to hide the king of hearts. Make sure that the king of hearts is on top of the squared packet before replacing it back on the table to the right of the T formation.

Note: Be sure to display all the packets in the same fashion, so as not to look suspicious.

Step 5: Now, you are going to apparently show that all four kings have joined the leader packet (Order from top to bottom should be in this: king of clubs, king of spades, jack of spades, jack of diamonds, and king of diamonds). Pick up the face down leader packet and turn the single top card (king of clubs) face up. Then, turn it face down and deal it on top of table. Now, transfer and turn over the bottom three cards squared as a triple face up sideways from bottom to top of packet. Show the king of diamonds face up. Use your right thumb to cover the suit of diamonds. Do a Triple Turnover by turning them face down squared on top of packet. Deal off a single face down card from the packet onto the first card dealt to the table. Finally, turn over the rest of the cards face up to show only the king of spades with the left hand and the king of diamonds as a double (with the jack of diamonds behind it) with the right hand. Place the king of spades and king of diamonds (double card) face down on top of the two cards on table one at a time. Be careful not to spread the double card as you lay them on the table.

Note: As you are apparently showing each king, don't call attention to the suits of each king.

Step 6: Everyone will assume that you've finished performing the routine. With the right hand arch over, pick up the leader packet still facing down. Buckle and get a little finger break above the king of clubs from bottom of the packet. You are going to use the same hand to pick up the middle packet and add the king of clubs on top of it **(See Figure # 22 & 23)**. After you secretly add the king of clubs, turn the two packets (middle and leader packets) face up with each hand. Pivot your right hand downwards and drop the leader packet squared face down onto the table in the same position of the T formation.

Note: This type of action needs to take place casually, as if you have finished the routine. You want to act as if you are squaring the packets and not to draw attention while secretly loading the king of clubs on top on top of the middle packet.

Step 6: Now, you are getting ready to create the illusion of three kings jumping back to their piles. Now, casually deal off the bottom card (jack of spades) from the packet with the left hand as you use this card to point to the rest of the packets of the T formation. Explain that you've caused three kings jump to the leader packet, except for the king of spades. Replace this card face down on top of the leader packet.

Step 8: Slightly spread the leader packet, with the faces to the left, so you don't expose the suits of the jacks; rather, only show the tips of the letters. Because the jack of diamonds and the jack of spades are on top of the packet, it will create the illusion that they are the other two kings, since the spectators will see the partial side of the faces. This was originally created by Darrin Martineau , which is called the Mis-Pip Display **(See Figure # 24)**.

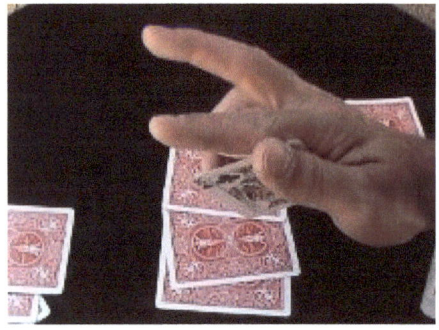

Figure # 22

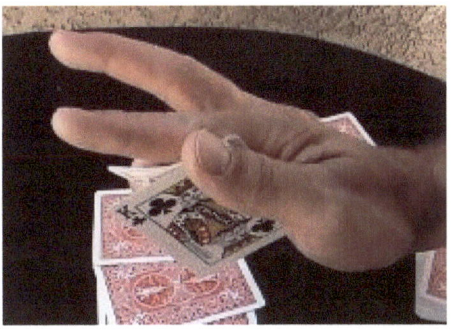

Figure # 23

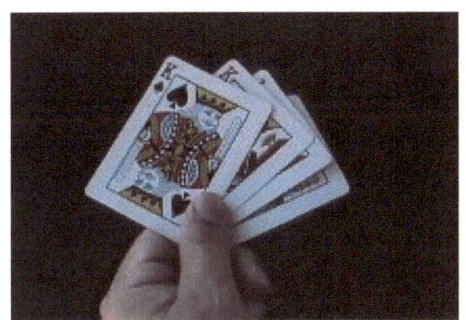

Figure # 24

Step 9: Transfer and turnover the two bottom cards face up, squared off the packet as one sideways (king of spades & king of diamonds) over on top of the leader packet to show the king of spades. The king of spades is second position from top of packet. Double Turnover the two cards face down. Explain that you haven't caused the last king to jump yet. Deal the top card (king of diamonds) face down (apparently the king of spades) on top of the left packet of the T formation. Say, "Watch!" Turn over the king of spades from the leader packet to show that it jumped back. Now explained that the kings are like magic "King"aroos because the other three have also magically jumped back to the piles. Turn over each king face up from the packets **(See Figure # 25)**.

Note: Keep your leader packet squared, since now there are only two face down cards. You can pick it up still squared with the face up king of spades on top, and place it on top of the deck before the spectators could examine all the cards afterwards. Also, you will noticed that the sequence of the kings on each pile at the end of the routine will be different than the beginning when you displayed them (right before you did the Multiple Turnover), and deal them from left to right: T formation. However, it's important for you not to indicate each suit throughout the entire routine. But rather you are simply stating them as the kings. And the time- delay between the beginning and ending is long.

The reason why the king of hearts is the right card of the T formation is because you want to leave one red king (king of diamonds) in the leader packet, since it creates a better illusion when apparently showing five cards as all four kings joined in one pile by dropping onto the table one at a time, which is more appealing.

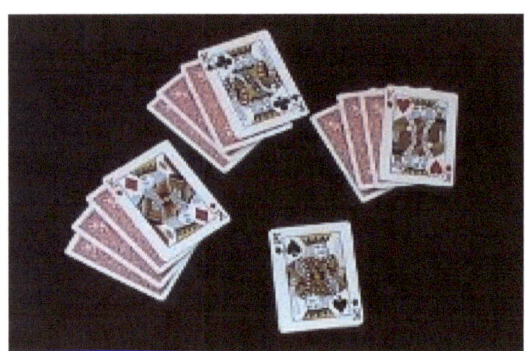

Figure # 25

A Wild Royal

An adaptation and inspired by of Darwin Ortiz's Jumping Gemini.

Effect: Each of the four aces turn into the selection card (ten of spades) after the selected card was placed on tabled at all times. Then, they all changed to the jack, queen, and king of spades for a royal flush.

Secret/Setup

From top of the deck, setup up in this order of the suit spade: king, ten, queen, and jack. Place the four aces face up on the table. The ace of spades is the first top card of the spread (not bottom of spread).

Method

Step 1: Cut the deck, keeping a little finger break between the two piles with the right hand. Execute a Riffle Force by asking a spectator to stop you, as you riffle the upper right corner with the right thumb. When stopped, bring the piles back to the original position. Execute a Double Turnover to show the ten of spades face up on the top of the deck, then turn double face down onto the pack. Deal the single top face down card (king of spades) to the center of the table.

Step 2: Spread the top three cards (ten of spades, queen of spades, and the jack of spades) and re-square the cards, catching a little finger break underneath them. With the left hand, pick up the aces from the table and place them face up, on top of the deck. Arch the left hand over and lift the entire packet of seven cards above the break (known as the Biddle Grip).

Step 3: Now, you are going to do J.K. Hartman's Secret Subtraction. Use your right thumb to deal off the first ace from the side and use the left- hand packet to flip the first ace face-down. Transfer it to the bottom of the left- hand packet, but the left thumb holds a flesh break between the first ace and the six cards above it **(See Figure # 26)**. You can rotate the left hand to show the first ace. Repeat this for the two other aces. Right before you deal out the ace of spades, secretly drop the face-down aces beneath the packet (below the thumb break) back on top of the deck **(See Figure #27)**. The ace of spades is still being transferred in the same fashion by going underneath the left-hand packet. Now, the order of the face- down left- hand packet from the top is: ten of spades, queen of spades, the jack of spades, and the ace of spades. Place the deck aside on the table.

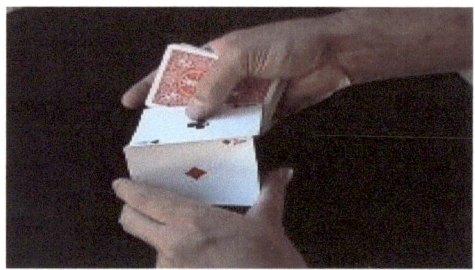

Figure # 26

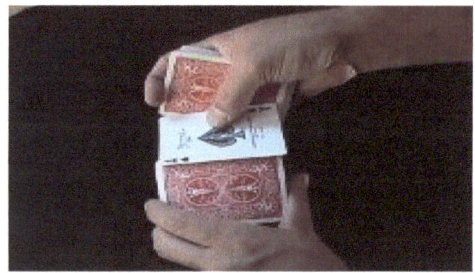

Figure # 27

Step 4: The ten of spades needs to be in the third position from the top of packet. You can do this while spreading the cards between your hands as a magical gesture right after you slide the top card to the third position with your right thumb, or simply say that you are shuffling them. **(See Figure # 28)**. Gather the cards back together as a packet. From the top of the face-down packet, the order of the cards should be: queen of spades, jack of spades, ten of spades, and the ace of spades.

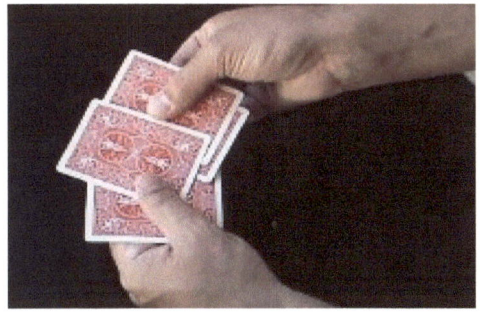

Figure # 28

Step 5: Now, you are ready to create an illusion that each of the four aces has turned into the selected card (ten of spades). Hold the packet face down with the right hand in a gambler's dealing position. With the right little finger, buckle the bottom card and keep a break between the bottom and third card. Turn over the top three cards squared face up as one (Triple Turnover) to show the ten of spades. Repeat the Triple Turnover, turning the Triple face down. Transfer the single top face down card (apparently the ten of spades) to the left hand. Hold it with the left thumb on top and fingers below. Repeat by buckling the bottom card with the right little finger, and use the first top card held in the left hand to turn over the two cards as a double face up (Double Turnover) to show the ten of spades again. This type of variation is called Diminishing Lift.

For the third time, use the previous method to simply turn (use the cards held in the left hand to flip) the single ten of spades face up, then back face down on top of the bottom card. Grip the bottom two cards, with the right thumb resting on top right side, and first two fingers on bottom right side. Simultaneously, use your first and second fingers to slide the bottom card (ace of spades) to underneath the bottom two cards held in the left hand while griping the ten of spades with the right two fingers. This is Larry Jennings's subtlety: apparently sliding the third card to underneath the other three cards, switching it for the bottom card, in order to make it look like the bottom card is also the ten of spades. **(See Figure # 29).**

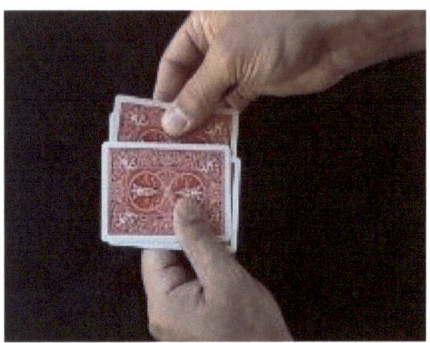

Figure # 29

Step 6: Now, you are going to do a Mexican Turnover to show that the tabled card is still the ten of spades, while actually the king of spades. Hold the ten of spades with the right thumb resting on top right side and first two fingers underneath the bottom right side. You are going to use this card to tilt upwards under the right inner edge of tabled card (king of spades). As the king of spades starts to slide under the tabled card, slightly lift the right thumb and transfer to the same position on the back of the king of spades as you turn the ten of spades face up, keeping the other card face down **(See Figure # 30, 31, & 32 for sequence of the switch).**

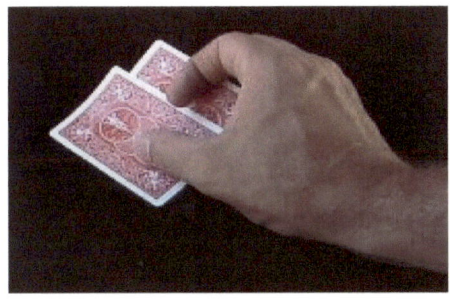

Figure # 30

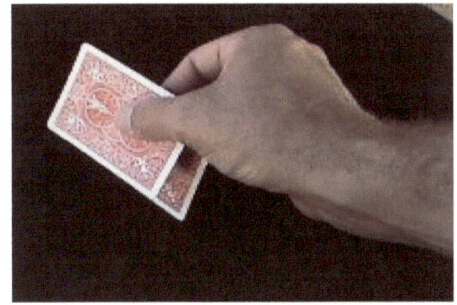

Figure # 31

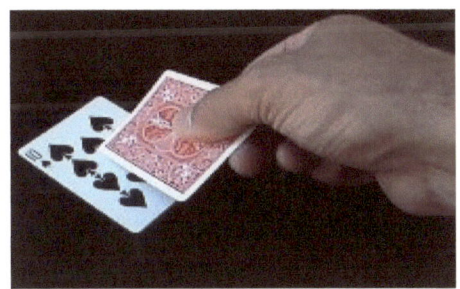

Figure # 32

As you are doing the entire slight, you say, "All four aces have changed to your selected card, the ten of spades". Keeping the king of spades face-down in your right hand, use it to scoop underneath the ten of spades (now on the table), and turn it face down onto the table. Drop the face down king of spades on top of the face down ten of spades, then drop the entire face down packet on top of them (king of spades & ten of spades).

Step 7: To reinforce that they are all ten of spades, use a Bro. John Hammon's Flushtration Count. Biddle grip the face down packet with the right hand. Rotate the packet face up to show the ten of spades on the bottom of packet, and rotate back downwards. Immediately, use the left thumb to slide the top card off into the left hand. Repeat this four more times in a smooth, even fashion manner. This will give the illusion that you've shown that all the cards are the ten of spades. Say, "If we were playing poker, then all of these ten of spades wouldn't be useful for a winning hand… instead it's better to have a royal flush." Place the ten of spades face up on table and turn over the rest of cards to show the rest of the royal flush. Deal the bottom two cards on to table one at a time, then drop the rest together. You are doing this type of display, in order to show the correct order of the royal flush: from ten to ace of spades slightly spread on table.

A Wild Royal (Version 2) (Read variation 1 first before reading this)

This is the same effect. However, for the surprise ending, all cards, including the ten of spades changed to a different suit: hearts for a royal flush.

Secret/Setup

From the top of the deck, set up the cards in this order: ten of hearts, ten of spades, jack of hearts, queen of hearts, and the king of hearts. Place the aces face up on the table, off to the side. The ace of hearts is the top card.

Method

Step 1: Do a Riffle Force and bring the original piles back together. Then do a Double Turnover to show the ten of spades. Turn Double face down. Place the top card (ten of hearts) on the center of table.

Step 2: Slightly spread the top four cards and re-square them, but keep a right little finger break under the top four cards. Pick up the face up aces from the table with the left hand, and place them still face up on top of the deck. With the left hand arched over the pack, lift off all the cards above the break, as a block.

Step 3: Use J.K. Hartman's Secret Subtraction by keeping the ace of hearts on the bottom of the left-hand packet with the rest of aces on top of the deck.

Step 4: Transfer the ten of spades to the second position from the bottom of packet. While keeping the packet squared, deal the ten of spades and the second card (jack of hearts) to the bottom of packet one at a time. As you are subtlety doing this, simply state that the cards are not marked or mention the color of the backs. The order from the top of the packet should now be this: queen of hearts, king of hearts, ace of hearts, ten of spades, and the jack of hearts.

Step 5: Use the Diminishing Lift to show that all of them have changed to the selected card (ten of spades). Be careful not to spread the bottom two cards. Keep them squared as a double, since you are apparently using only four cards. For the last two cards, snap them as a double while pinching them with the right thumb on top right side and first two fingers on bottom right side. I perform Larry Jenning's version, using the three dealt cards from the left hand to cover the bottom card while switching it to show the last card, which is the ten of spades. The first three dealt cards from the left hand should be spread in a fan, so it can easily cover the fourth card (jack of hearts). After you've shown the single ten of spades, you can now square the whole packet.

Step 6: Use the Mexican Turnover to show the ten of spades from the table. (Same technique from version 1). Then, turn over the ten of spades face down, and drop the face down ten of hearts on top of ten of spades. Finally, drop the remaining face down squared packet on top of the two cards on table.

Step 7: Use the Flushtration Count to show all to be the ten of spades, but keep the two cards together as a double (ten of spades and ten of hearts). Place the double on top of the rest of packet face up as one and hold the packet together with the right hand in a gambler's dealing position. Do a Double Turnover. Deal off the top card face up, then hold it with the left hand to show that the ten of spades have changed to the ten of hearts. While keeping the ten of hearts face up, buckle the second and third card of packet with the right little finger and use the ten of hearts to turnover them over, face up, as one. The jack of hearts will be showing. Keep them as a double next to the ten of hearts as you continue showing the rest of cards by turning them face up one at a time. Be careful not to spread the jack of hearts and ten of spades while you are holding the spread of royal flush with the right hand.

Note: You could have the ten of spades signed and palmed off from the top of the deck after the effect. This way, you can use any of your favorite card revelation, including the card to wallet, in a card box, or simply a card in pocket method.

Magnus Opus Travelers

This is an adaptation of Don England's Open Travelers. I would like to thank Darin Martineau for helping me in creating this adaptation. Larry Jennings originally created the effect called "Invisible Palm/Open Travelers". It's a concept of causing three aces to become invisible and magically appear one at a time on top of the tabled ace. Don England created a variation, which he starts off with four aces, they then all turned to the four kings at the end as a surprise finale.

This routine starts with four jacks. After they all change to the four aces, the jacks reappeared in four different pockets. The revelation of each jack appearing in four different pockets is an inspiration of Dr. Jacob's Gambler vs. Magician's finale and Dai Vernon's variation of four aces from four different pockets routine.

Secret/Setup

Preset two jacks in two different pockets: the jack of clubs is in your left breast pocket of your jacket and the jack of hearts is in your left pocket of your pants.

Set the packet of five cards in this order face-down: ace of clubs, jack of diamonds, ace of hearts, ace of diamonds, and jack of spades.

Method

Step 1: Hold the packet of five cards squared with your right hand. You can spread as four cards by keeping the bottom two cards squared as a double.

Step 2: Now, you are going to apparently show as four jacks of each suit while displaying them one at a time. This is a variation of Larry Jennings's Rhythm Count. With the face down packet squared in your right hand, perform a Double Turnover to show the jack of diamonds, but cover the suits with the whole base of your thumb. Don't mention its suit, simply refer to it as a jack **(See Figure # 33)**.

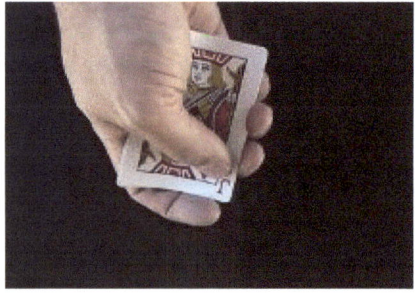

Figure # 33

Step 3: Double Turnover the cards again and deal the first card to the table with the right thumb. Then immediately deal the next face down second card (jack of diamonds) of the packet to the left hand using the same right thumb. Turn over your right hand while keeping the rest of the cards squared to show the jack of spades on the bottom of the packet, as you use the upper right corner face down jack of diamonds from the left hand to cover the upper left corner suit of jack of spades. Remember to not mention its suit; call it as a second jack **(See Figure # 34).**

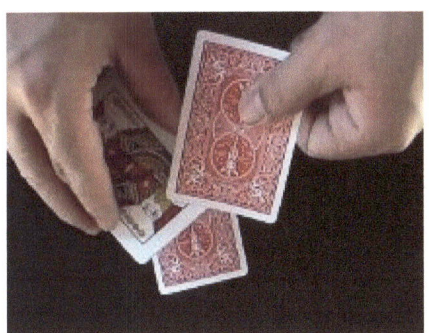

Figure # 34

Step 3: Turn your right hand over in a swinging motion again to deal out the top face down card ace of hearts of the right-hand packet (apparently the jack of spades) with your right thumb on top of the first dealt (ace of clubs) card on table. Now, the jack of spades and ace of diamonds are held with your right hand as a double. Turn the jack of diamonds face up with the left hand as you simultaneously turn the double card over face up (jack of spades showing) with the right hand. Place the jack of diamonds on top of the face up double card (the jack of spades). Square them as a packet and turn it face down. Deal off the top card (ace of diamonds) on top of the spread of the two aces face down. Still hold the jack of diamonds and jack of spades as a face down double (jack of diamonds showing) with the right hand,

and lay it them face down parallel next to the three cards on the table **(See Figure # 35).**

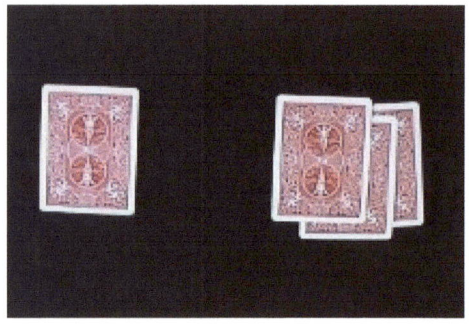

Figure #35

(double card to the left (jack of diamonds & jack of spades); three aces or "jacks" to the right (from audience's view)

 Note: If done correctly without hesitation and without recalling its suits, you've apparently shown as all four jacks one at a time.

Step 4: Pick up the three cards and hold them with the left hand. Now, you are going to create the illusion that you will make those three "jacks" invisibly transfer to the leader jack on the table. Keeping the first top card face down, tilt it at about a 45 degree angle by holding it with the left thumb on the top side(with the face toward you). Your right hand approaches and covers that card. The right thumb goes behind the card (A Paul Harris's Variation) **(See Figure # 36).** This is known as a Tent Vanish.

As soon as you cover the tilted card, you move your right thumb over it quickly, and allow it to fall aligned on top of the other two cards held in your left hand. Act as if you are palming it off invisibly from the left hand by keeping your right fingers together. Show the palm of your right hand by rotating it, in order to give the impression that it's "invisible".

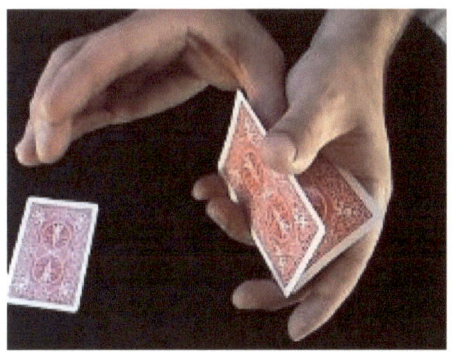

Figure # 36 (side view)

Step 5: As your right hand approaches to the double card from the table, use the heel of the right hand to separate the cards before spreading the fingers and gesturing from left to right, rather than looking like you simply spread them **(See Figure # 37 and 38).**

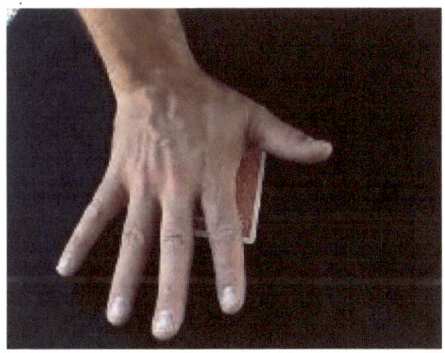

Figure # 37

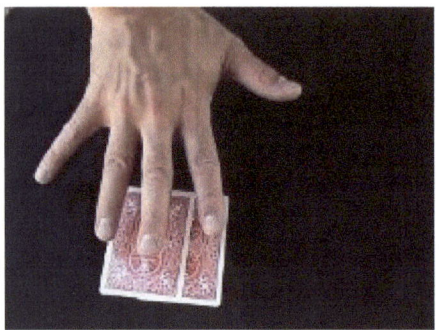

Figure # 38

Step 6: With the right hand arch over (Biddle Grip) the packet of three cards from left hand, deal out the bottom two cards off to the right side as a double with the right thumb on inner side and second right finger on upper side of the cards .The double card overlaps the single card as you lay them down on the table parallel next the other two single cards (jack of diamonds & jack of spades) to the right. **(See Figure # 39).**

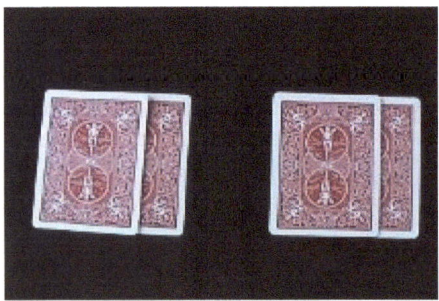

Figure # 39 (three cards as two to the right from audience's view)

Step 7: Now, you are going to use Allan Ackerman's Open Packet Switch by using a time delay misdirection. Give at least a ten second time delay by showing your hands empty, and pick up the two single cards from the table, as if you are using the same cards you've previously used. Don't recall the same cards you had previously; casually pick up the cards and continue with for the Tent Vanish for the third "jack".

Step 8: Repeat the Tent Vanish method **(same as Figure # 33)** for the two single cards (jack of diamonds & jack of spades) by dropping the tilted card aligned on top of the other single card from the left hand. Approach the open right hand palm down and use its heel to separate the cards on table to magically show the third card **(See Figure # 40).**

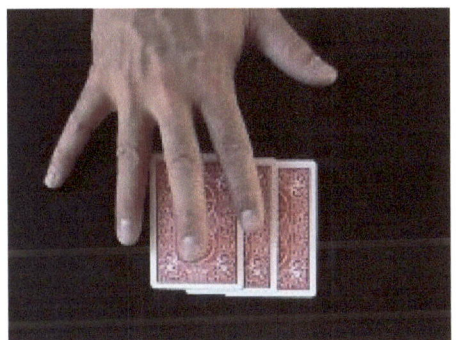

Figure # 40

Step 9: Keep the two cards (jack of diamonds & jack of spades) as a double with your left hand. You can twirl, or snap it together with the two first fingers and thumb, in order to give the impression that you have only one card. Then place the double card face up horizontally next to the three face down spread cards **(See Figure # 41).**

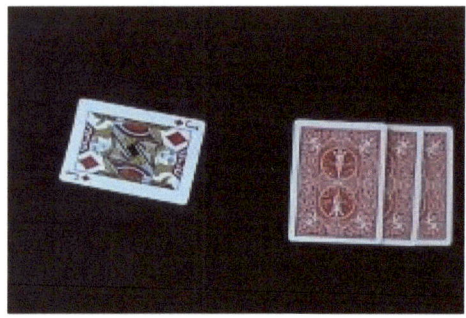

Figure # 41 (from audience's view)

Step 10: Pick up the face up deck with your right hand. Now, you are going to execute a Turn-Over Change (Inspired by Rene Lavand's book, *Magic from the Soul*) to switch out the double card (jack of diamonds & jack of spades) for the ace of spades on top of the deck. Explain that you could have used any four of a kind from the deck as you pick up and show the deck, since you want to give a logical reason why you picked it up from the side of the table. Hold the deck in a face down dealing position. As you turn over your right hand, allow the top card (ace of spades) to tilt slightly by squeezing your second, third, and fourth fingers on the deck. Approach the double card and slide the ace of spades underneath them. Make sure that the ace of spades is aligned with the double card before you turn your right hand over again. Use your right thumb to deal off the ace of spades face down onto the table next to the other three face down cards. Replace the deck on table. **(See Figure # # 42, 43, & 44 for sequence of the Turn-Over Switch).**

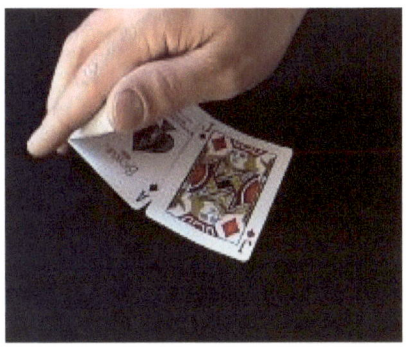

Figure # 42

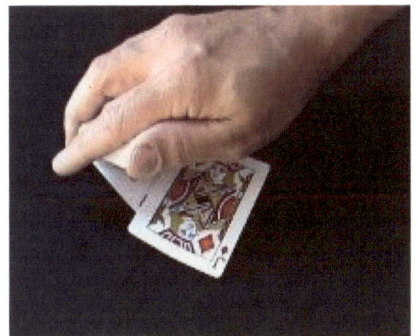

Figure # 43

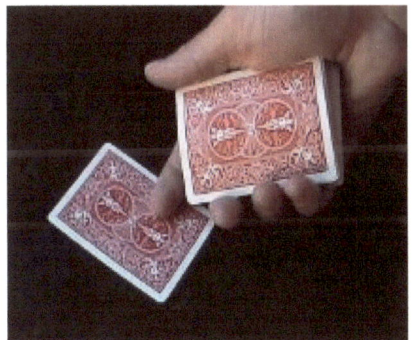

Figure # 44

Step 11: Explain that you attempting to make the last card invisible by placing your right palm over it, then wave it in a magical gesture. After couple times of attempts, finally explain that not only you can make them invisible, but change them to a better four of a kind. Reveal the four aces **(See Figure # 45)**.

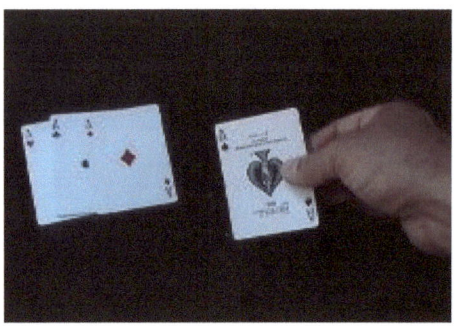

Figure # 45

Step 12: Now you are going to reveal all four jacks from four different pockets. Pick up the face down deck with your left hand in a gambler's dealing position. Palm off the jack of diamonds & jack of spades from the top of the deck with your right hand.

Step 13: Replace the deck on the table with the left hand. Make sure that your left hand looks like your right hand with the palm cards. Act as if you are searching for the four jacks by patting on the front side of your body with your palms one at a time. Turn your left shoulder slightly to the right, and use your left hand to pull the preloaded jack of clubs out of your left breast pocket of your jacket. At the same time, you drop the jack of diamonds from your right palm into your outer right pocket of your jacket, while keeping the other jack of spades still palmed.

Place the face up jack of clubs on the table with the left hand as you reach your right palm with the jack of spades into your right pocket of your pants to reveal it. Then, use your left hand to pull the preloaded jack of hearts out of the left pocket of your pants. Finally, use your right hand to reveal the jack of diamonds from your outer right pocket of your jacket.

Note: The whole sequence of this four jack's revelation from four different pockets should be done smoothly in rhythm without any hesitation.

Basic Card Sleights
For Beginners

Hindu Shuffle

Hindu Shuffle Force

Hindu Shuffle Control

The Double Lift & Turnover

The Buckle

Palming

The Elmsley Count

Hindu Shuffle

The Hindu Shuffle is one of the basic shuffles that has many purposes, such as the use of forcing cards, controlling, and glimpsing. Hold the inner end of the deck face down with your right thumb and second finger. Use your left fingers to pull a small portion of cards (approximately eight to twelve cards) from the top of the deck, and drop them on your left open palm. Continue until you've dealt off all of the cards from your right hand in a fashion manner **(See Figure # 46 & 47)**. You could also do the Hindu Shuffle with the cards being face up.

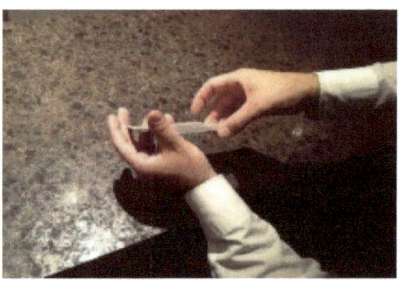

Figure # 46

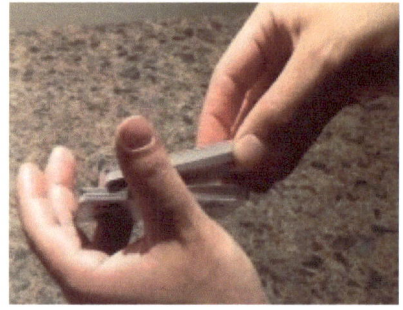

Figure # 47

A Hindu Shuffle Force

To force a card, as if the card was freely selected, you ask to stop while you use the Hindu Shuffle. When stopped, simply show them the bottom card of the remaining pile from your right hand (if you are doing this with cards being face down) or the top card (if you are doing this with the cards being face up), as if it was randomly selected (**See Figure 48 & 49).** If you force the top card as shown from Figure #49, then turn your right hand around and deal the top on the table face down with your right thumb. This is very useful for most of the color changing deck variations.

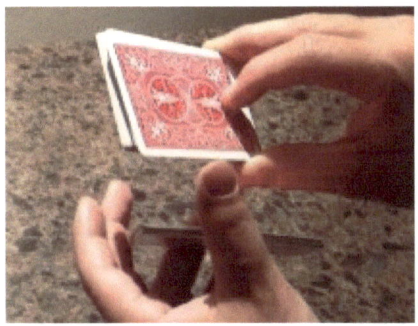

Figure # 48

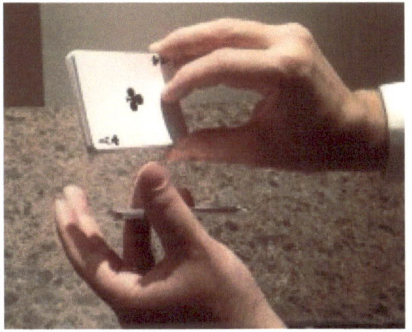

Figure # 49

Hindu Shuffle Control

Have a card freely selected. As you do the Hindu shuffle with approximately half the cards drawn to the left hand, ask to place the selected card on top of these cards. When you bring your right hand-packet toward the left- hand packet (with the selected card on top of the left- hand packet), continue the Hindu Shuffle while keeping a thumb break between the outer edges of the two halves **(See Figure # 50)**. Continue the shuffle until you get above the break. Drop the remaining cards on top of the others held in the left hand, so the selected card is now on top of the deck.

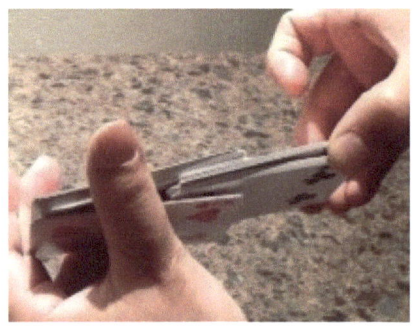

Figure # 50

Note: You could actually do this with each ace or your favorite four of a kind one at a time.

The Double Lift & Turnover

The Double Lift and Turnover, in my opinion, the best card slight that every card magician uses. It's a technique that allows you to lift off two cards over as a double from either on top of the deck or a small packet of cards.

Hold the deck face down with the left hand in a dealer's position. With the right hand, use your thumb to riffle the inner end of cards from the middle until you reach to the second card from top of the deck. Then, use your first and second fingers to grip the two cards as one, as you turn them over face up on top of the deck **(See Figure # 51)**. This is called as a Double Turnover. Show the apparent top card, perform a Double Turnover again, and show the very single top card face up, as if it magically changed to the selected card. This could be a very good follow up after you've controlled the selected card using the Hindu Shuffle Control (See pg. 48). You could also create an illusion that the apparent card magically rose to the top of the deck after inserting into the center of the deck.

Note: You could perform a Triple or Quadruple Lift and Turnover (preferably 4 or 5).

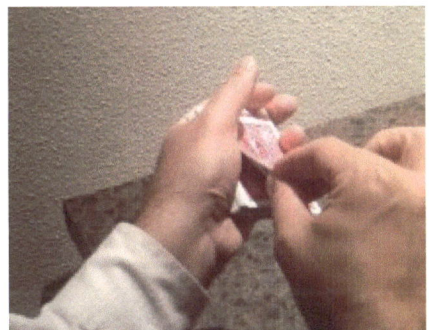

Figure # 51

The Buckle

The Buckle is very useful, particularly for a small packet of cards while either executing a double triple lift with a small packet, a false count, or glimpsing a card. For example, with the packet face down, the right fourth finger pulls the inner left corner of the second card toward the base of the thumb. A gap is created underneath this second card, allowing the right, fourth finger to retain the break **(See Figure # 52).**

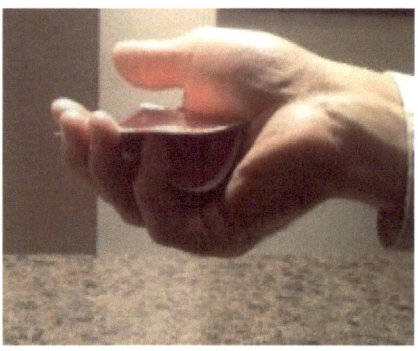

Figure # 52

Palming

This type of variation is very useful for many purposes, such as producing either a selected card or multiple cards from any type of pocket and replacing back onto the deck after shuffled by a spectator. Get a little finger break under the top card or two cards as you arch your right hand over the deck, and grip with the all four fingers on outer side and thumb inner side of it. Move your left hand upwards slightly, using the fingers and thumb to push the two cards up against the right palm of your right hand while keeping the right fingers close together **(See Figure # 53).**

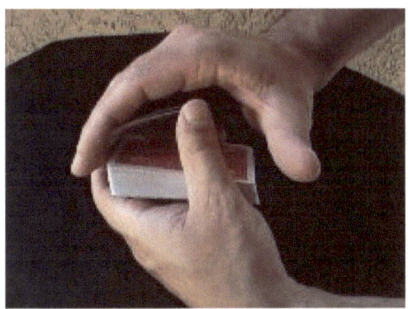

Figure # 53

The Elmsley Count

The Elmsley Count is one of the useful and popular secret counts, which four cards are openly counted while secretly concealing any number of cards, either face up or down.

Let's assume that we are using four cards, which the third card from the top packet is face- up. Hold and pinch the packet with the right thumb on top of the center right long edge and rest of fingers from underneath. Slide off the top card to the left thumb and first fingers and hold on the center of the left long edge while you move your right hand back to the right. When you move your right hand back to the left again, slide off the next two cards aligned together above the first dealt card while simultaneously retrieve the first top dealt card back to underneath the bottom card that is still held with the right thumb and first fingers **(See Figure # 54)**.

Slide off the rest of the cards to the left hand. This action creates the illusion that you've counted four face down cards to the left hand while hiding the face up card.

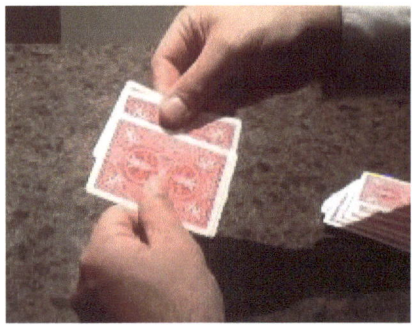

Figure # 54

Note: You could also execute this sleight to count three cards as four.

Bibliography

Card Magic by Jean Northern Hilliard

Counts, Cuts, and Subtlety by Jerry Mentzer

Las Vegas Kardma by Allan Ackerman

Magic from the Soul by René Lavand

Royal Road to Card Magic by Jean Hugard and Frederick Braue

The New Modern Coin Magic by J.B. BoBo